Dear Regime

Dear Regime

Letters to the Islamic Republic

poems

Roger Sedarat

OHIO UNIVERSITY PRESS

ATHENS

Ohio University Press, Athens, Ohio 45701
www.ohio.edu/oupress
© 2008 by Ohio University Press

Printed in the United States of America
All rights reserved

Ohio University Press books are printed on acid-free paper ⊗ ™

16 15 14 13 12 11 10 09 08   5 4 3 2 1

Library of Congress Cataloging-in-Publication Data
Sedarat, Roger, 1971–
  Dear Regime : letters to the Islamic republic : poems / Roger Sedarat.
    p. cm.
  ISBN-13: 978-0-8214-1774-4 (cloth : acid-free paper)
  ISBN-10: 0-8214-1774-6 (cloth : acid-free paper)
  ISBN-13: 978-0-8214-1775-1 (pbk. : acid-free paper)
  ISBN-10: 0-8214-1775-4 (pbk. : acid-free paper)
  1. Iran—Poetry. I. Title.
  PS3619.E33D43 2007
  811'.6—dc22
                              2007033710

Acknowledgments

Poems in this collection appeared originally in the following publications: *Atlanta Review* ("Ghost Story," "I Watched You Braiding Persian Violets into Your Hair," and "Thigh"); *Plainsongs* ("Dear Regime,"); *Hanging Loose* ("Advertisement Proposal," "Permissible Grapes, Forbidden Wine," "Athletes Make the Best Persian Pornography," and "Cousin Farzad's Wedding"); *Iranian.com* ("Iranian Darwins"); *The Ledge* ("Eating Chelo at Aunt Behjat's in Tehran"); *New England Review* ("Essential Journey"); *Visions International* ("Qormeh Sabzi"); *Hayden's Ferry Review* ("Khomeini's Beard"); *Raw Nervz* ("Persian Haiku"); *The Hat* ("The Hysterical Is Historical" and "Picnic"); *Poet Lore* ("Agha D—"). The author also wishes to acknowledge a St. Botolph Club Foundation poetry grant-in-aid as well as four successive work-study scholarships to the Bread Loaf Writers' Conference that supported the writing of this manuscript.

For now, come night,
not only has he lost all his fear,
now he goes out
just looking for trouble.

—Hafez

Contents

Part A(s If Change Were Possible)

Ghost Story   3

Dear Regime,   4
Body Cleaner   5
In Praise of Moths   7
Agha D—   19
I Watched You Braiding Persian Violets into Your Hair   20
Calligraphy   21
Cousin Farzad's Wedding   23
At the Firing Squad   25
Athletes Make the Best Persian Pornography   26
Satellite of Love   27
AK, a Figurehead of the Revolution, Interviews the Author   29
Eating Chelo at Aunt Behjat's in Tehran   31
Prelude to a Blackout   32
Iranian Darwins   33
At the Hezbollah Recruiting Station   34
Dear Regime (Letters toward a Revolution)   35
Revolutionary Reflections   36

Part B(ut Poetry Doesn't Make Revolutions)

Essential Journey   39
Flying to Persia   41
Dowsing   42

Qormeh Sabzi   44

Khomeini's Beard   46

Doctor   47

Thigh   49

Haji as Stick Figure   50

Permissible Grapes, Forbidden Wine   51

This Little Haji   52

Jun   53

Adidas   54

Persian Haiku   55

Haji's Rubaiyyat   56

When Haji Comes to Town   58

Advertisement Proposal   59

The Hysterical Is Historical: An Interview with Haji   60

Farrokhzad's Paper Hat   63

Haji as Street Urchin   64

Haji's Garden   65

If a Body Catches Haji   66

Picnic   68

Tanboor   69

Reinstatement of the Rose   71

Part C(ontextual Notes)   75

Part A(s If Change Were Possible)

Ghost Story

By the time said country gets the bomb
my infant son will read the news.
For now I merely crackle each page
of the paper before him, if only
to shake myself from reality.
How often this boy (descendent of said country)
saves me from terrifying thoughts of the future.
Just yesterday while washing a month's worth of laundry
I became a magician, pulling sheets upon sheets
from a single container, as if to trick him
into believing that things are eternal.
Then when I laid his two-foot-tall body
upon a sea of freshly dried clothes,
he showed me how little we matter,
enshrouding himself in a white cotton sheet
for his mock-Muslim burial.
I remembered the morning's story
and he began shaking himself free.
Tiny ghost of the symbolic, insistent snickerdoodle
intent on making life meaningful,
go forth in the world with your blankness,
cover that which becomes too scary to see,
take back your first word as soon as it's spoken,
and so haunt the world as a prophet of innocence.

Dear Regime,

After you've ground him into powder,
you can burn this to a fine ash. His family feels
it would be better off with nothing.

My father returned from Iran with everything but his bones.
He said customs claimed them as government property.
We laid him on a Persian carpet in front of the television.
When I'd hold his wrist to his face
because he wanted to know the time,
we could see the holes made by swords in his elbow.
His arm reminded me of *kebab kubideh.*
It was hard for him to look outside;
he said the cumulus clouds
were too much like marrow
and he couldn't stand watching the dog
sniff the backyard, searching
for the rest of him. My sister and I put him to bed
thinking that beside our mother
he'd turn into himself,
but through the door we only heard him crying,
telling his wife he could never again make love,
and through the keyhole we saw her shivering with him
wrapped around her like an old blanket
until he died one morning.
She folded him into a rectangle,
mailing him in a white shoebox
back to his country.

Body Cleaner

My cousin Miriam's friend,
let's call her "Azadeh"
(meaning "freedom"),
prepares women for execution,
washing bodies and brushing hair
on the last night of their lives.
I hear they eat a simple meal
of cheese, bread, and fresh greens
before lying on a sofa
in a room with no windows
waiting to be informed of the morning
much like they were told of their crimes
and taken to prison,
then this place
where rosemary-scented olive oil
reminds them of the body's limitation,
the feet carrying them only so far,
the hands reaching for God
coming up empty.

Azadeh takes photographs of each one
wrapped in her white burial sheet.
I wanted to send copies to the *New York Times*,
but it would put certain people in danger,
so instead I put it in this poem
hoping that at least one reader
stops long enough

to think about the burden
of living in a world
with death sentences.

In Praise of Moths

I

From seeds in an oversized suitcase
shell-colored moths unpack their wings
and begin consuming contents of the closet.

My father-in-law came for his grandson's birth
but ended up dying of cancer
a week after the boy was born.

How quickly the cells turned against him.
The moths had scarcely touched his clothes
before he started to waste away.

We sent his body back to Iran
with a plane full of mourners.
Grief consumed my wife like cancer,

even as our son learned to open his eyes
and study the world
where all things live and die,

learning to crawl in his grandfather's house,
where we opened the closet door
to a blizzard of moths

and he gasped in delight
at insects capable of devouring
his favorite wool blanket.

II

Prayer for plague to gnaw at the threads
woven into Persian carpets,

an almighty erasure of domesticated game
appearing on each family's living room floor,

decay of cornucopia upon which the gaze
feeds for hours at afternoon *mehmunis*.

In the name of the most compassionate and merciful
bleach all money exchanged at the bazaar.

Let the people sleep in real forests and fields.
Let the starving frogs in the *jub* grow fat

upon moths who make us see again.
Let each mosque's microphone flutter

with wing-beats in the crisp autumn air;
Let the moon attract the deep desire

for our own country's timely death
where mullahs' beards breed moths by the hour.

III

The censor limited each poet to a single line.

The political one wrote, "You are cutting our throats."

The one full of love merely printed the name of his beloved.

The religious one cited the Koran.

The literary historian said, "Read Hafez."

The dying one killed moths in his room.

The Shah's son implored the reader to recall his father.

The musician scribbled a few spontaneous notes.

The illiterate gardener drew a picture of the nightingale.

The mullah wrote and published an entire book.

The opium addict mumbled, "Life is a dream."

The graphic designer cut and pasted advertisement slogans.

The woman on trial spelled her name with charcoal and
tears.

The children of the dying one wiped moth guts off the wall.

IV

Moths circle moonlit mosques' gold minarets.
An anti-U.S. speech hangs in the air.
My wife's American. She almost forgets,
At times, to completely cover her hair.
"Inglisi sobhat nakon," says Babak
(Don't speak English). We're near where my dad lived
Before Iran killed him. When I get back
To the U.S. I'll expose the record
Of personal atrocities behind
The ornate Islamic forms, shine a light
On the chador to help hungry moths find
Thick fabric that keeps women locked inside.
The truth will surface from the suffering;
We'll walk naked with God (who's all seeing).

V

Now open your mouth, Iran, and guzzle
The imperative tense in this ghazal.

Sold oil, thick enough to choke a poet,
Censors by spilling across the ghazal.

The "glug glug" of booze in Muslim countries
Echoes through most mosques (the devil's ghazal).

In case you haven't noticed, I'm turning
Over forms. I'm starting with the ghazal.

My Uncle N— led SAVAK for the Shah,
A dead letter left inside this ghazal.

Most Persians worship "Hafez," but Hafez
Transcended his ego in the ghazal.

Double double boiling some trouble:
Eye of Khomeini plopped into a ghazal.

My Father's Buick, a real gas guzzler,
Backfired, and wrote its own kind of ghazal.

You're not supposed to be so postmodern
By saying, "Look, this poem's a ghazal."

We drank fizzy *doogh* on our road trip
Out of the bottle. It hurt to guzzle.

Behind the new nuclear power plant
Two lovers like two lines in a ghazal . . .

I will not put myself in this ghazal.
If you want me, you've read the wrong ghazal.

VI

The old country—
A tank rolls in,
sound of war.

VII

Grind the green police into a vegetable state.
Toss them like a salad in a satellite dish.
Grill the government over coals like kebab.
Catch the crooked bureaucracy like a fish.
"In the unconscious," writes Freud, "all is possible,"
hence this surreal death of a revolution.
The green police, to paraphrase Cheap Trick,
live inside of my head.
Look, up in the air . . . it's a bird . . . it's a plane . . .
It's the Twelfth Imam come to judge the world,
starting with Iran. Blindfolds, please. Guns loaded.
Cigars, cigarettes? For a last meal the soldiers
collectively dine on their deeds mashed like mutton
with an old Coke bottle, bubbly *abgusht*
on an August picnic with no shade,
only tanks filled with Shirazi roses.

VIII

To think I'm using the word qasida
For mono rhyme to write a qasida

Means either I don't like qasidas
Or I'm just a basket case. Idea

For Persian poetry: the qasida
Speaks for itself. "My name is qasida

And no one (in Persian *hich kas*) I'd ap-
prove of could make me change it: "Qasida."

The Persian essence. Not "quesadilla,"
A Mexican food fused with qasida.

This restaurant's serving only qasida.
Oh empire of decay, this qasida

Will not redeem you. It says "qasida"
To push you past the threshold. "Qasida!"

A revolution of one qasida
Before a million mirrors. "Qasida."

Duplicity in the news. "Qasida"
Transcribed in students' notebooks. "Qasida!"

Scream poets from unmarked graves. "Qasida!"
I saw my uncle murdered. Qasida.

They beat a girl for lipstick. "Qasida."
Blood drops on walls of the mosque. "Qasida."

A wine remade in Shiraz. Qasida.
And Hafez keeps writing his qasida.

This poem will never stop: qasida
Until people start chanting "Qasida!

Qasida qasida qasida q—"

IX

I went for a jog in Iran and hurt my knee.
It worked out well, because I kept yelling, "(k) Oh-my-knee!"

A moth goes into therapy for a stutter.
"I think I hate my moth . . . moth . . . mother."

I've been eating a lot of pistachios lately,
thinking, "That Ahmadinejad is a real nut."

My wife, she's so Iranian, we got audited
and she brought gifts to the IRS.

This moth's mother goes into a bar and says,
"My son's a real asshole."

Seriously folks, the Islamic Republic has a moral code.
You can have sex with a prostitute, but you have to get married.

Why do Iranians love the song "Row Row Row Your Boat"?
Because with all the opium they smoke, life is but a dream.

How many mullahs does it take to screw in a lightbulb?
One hundred: One to do the wiring, and the other ninety-
    nine to abuse the power.

Ahmadinejad's wife has this large dildo, and it runs on a battery.
No wonder he wants to get nuclear power.

Actually, Iran is a progressive country. Women's headscarves
now come in two colors: black and light black.

X

Dear Regime:

The trick to reading this kind of book
is to stop taking yourself so seriously
just because you find yourself the butt of a joke.

The hand of the poet, so present here,
waves playfully, welcoming you over to dinner
after your twenty-five-plus-year fast.

Don't chop it off just because it offends you.
Like the severed tail of the desert lizard,
it can move on its own.

"Grasp me in friendship," says the hand.
"Let's walk through these pages
and show the world the power of humanity."

With enough light and color, the gray moth
becomes a butterfly.
Take my hand. Let's go to the place

of empty buildings (neutral territory)
and write these words upon the facade:

"If we lived here, we'd be home by now."

Agha D —

When I meet the literary historian of a nation,
he's writing a book in his underwear,

cutting and pasting the faces of poets
into ruler-drawn boxes.

As he holds each black-and-white face before me,
he slices his throat with his index finger,

showing one regime in the old country
suffices as metaphor for another,

substitutions for fear the written word
with all its ambiguities

might lead others to question
positions of power.

Take this poem, for example, designed to frame
the missing men

who surreptitiously appear under the wand
of the critic's finger,

which also arrives as warning to me,
another poet in a chain of being

bound to struggle for his voice
across the censor's literal sword.

I Watched You Braiding Persian Violets into Your Hair

Hair like the oil from your country bubbling
in a world underground where exiled musicians
play to women without their chadors.

Hair of fire like Farrokhzad's words:
curled letters of Persian in India ink, the dip
of a primitive fountain pen writing forbidden verses
in the blank page of an old textbook.

Hair the length of a first kiss, a boy's trembling fingers
and the walk home past the garden
with the scent of mint and jasmine.

Hair the sound of the Caspian Sea at night,
the unconditioned break of each wave, and starlit sand
pouring from a lover's shoe like a Persian hourglass.

Calligraphy

I

Sent to the bathroom with a fresh razor,
I come out clean and lie on a concrete floor.
The words of God tickle between my fingers

where things always escape my grasp.
The words of love inside my ear
at last seem permanent. "Don't cry,"

warns the calligrapher. "The work will run."
Covered from head to toe in ancient text,
I'm ready for filming, a veiled object

subject to exposure. When finished,
she hands me soap and a towel.
I just ask for my shoes.

"It's too dangerous; I wish you'd
shower first," she says. I tell her I wish
she'd used a knife.

II

Waiting for a train in Tehran,
sweat on my body
smears my significance

like newspaper in the rain.
Pacing the platform, I'm made to perform
a dumb show. What does one do at the end

of meaning something to the world?
All eyes pass by me. In the middle of nowhere,
I unfold my hands

(clammy from hopeless prayer)
and swipe an X through words
that won't stop bleeding.

Cousin Farzad's Wedding

Soldiers show up uninvited, opening
presents before it gets started, keeping
silver platters for their wives. They

are so happy that before confiscating
the cassettes of Persian music, they
let it play, even put down their rifles

to dance. One cuts the cake with his knife;
the icing clings to his beard as he looks
the bride up and down. You would think

he is her proud father if you don't notice
the bald gentleman burying his head
in his folded arms, refusing to pick up

the sword of *jujeh kebab* the lieutenant
holds above him. They collect a fine
of three thousand U.S. dollars from Farzad

and leave for vacation on the Caspian Sea,
but with true Persian hospitality, they
radio their friends at the barracks

with directions, so by the time more food
is on the table and the people begin
smiling again, the rest of the company

arrives, parking their jeeps on the lawn,
running to the door as if they are afraid,
by coming too late, they've missed all the fun.

At the Firing Squad

Another line of blindfolded men
facing the firing squad,
unable to return the studied gaze
of squinting soldiers.

A scene so familiar that the barest details—
tied hands behind the back, the order to aim—
suffice for verisimilitude.
Oh just another morality play,

this reporting of death sentences;
the writer knows it will not change a thing.
But what of the moment after the firing
and the clearing of smoke across mass graves,

now that the hunted got to pray
an *Allah-o Akbar* in the humblest of voices?
Are the executed granted a vision of paradise,
able to run with deer to the stream?

The question is almost pedantic in a world
requiring submission to one's government.
Whatever meaning the soul makes fails to matter.
So another poet writes more or less the same poem,

fully aware that words won't save people.
Print this on the thinnest of paper;
see that it's used to roll somebody's last cigarette
before the inevitable fall into the grave.

Athletes Make the Best Persian Pornography

Reza Goes Bowling. Banned in Iran as a sport
for its obvious sexual suggestions,
watch close-ups of this young man (who looks very much
like a Persian singer in his blue sequined suit)
putting three fingers in a red ball.

The Bicycle Ride through Shah-Goli Park. See Persian beauties
do a no-no in Shiraz by pedaling
on twenty-year-old Schwinns with banana seats
past gentlemen who watch from park benches.
See and hear Hishmet ring her silver bell!

A Game of Nasty 8-Ball. Three teenagers
sneak into a basement to shoot pool,
illegal behavior that's hotter than a stick of kebab.
A mustached Mohammad Mir even reaches
into a hole to retrieve the white ball.

Shirin Takes Up Swimming. This young woman
does the butterfly and breaststroke
in a blue bathing suit and polka-dotted
swimming cap. Check out the skin that chadors
have kept you missing. Her kneecaps are beautiful!

The Co-Ed Relay Race. Men and women,
for a second that gets replayed in slow motion,
actually touch hands while passing the baton.
You haven't seen anything this sexy since
the Shah and his wife played baseball.

Satellite of Love

On the black market, the man in the raincoat buys
a bikini and a blond wig. Swimming naked
in his pool later that day, he pretends to drown.

Out comes his 300-pound wife, squeezed
into neon pink top and bottom, her new hair
pulled a bit too far forward, to cover her brown eyes.

What do the neighbors behind the wall think
when they hear, "Save me, Pamela Anderson!"
and peek through the crack to see a blonde lifeguard?

What does the woman feel as she faces
a video camera while making love to her husband
who wears a white floating donut?

If the country were more liberal, perhaps she'd have
a support group for women affected by their husbands'
new addiction to American TV.

The butcher's wife, because her husband gets HBO,
would complain about 9 1/2 *Weeks*, her having
to pour last night's *fesenjan* and rice over her body.

Instead of setting fire to *The Satanic Verses*, imagine
a wig- and lingerie-burning party, the acrid smoke
filling the streets, like teargas in men's eyes.

As in pre-1979, a revolution's cooking; the woman
who plays Pamela beats an omelet in a metal bowl
so loud the neighbors call to complain.

The police chief's wife, when she's out in the garden
snipping mint and thyme, accidentally slips, cuts
through the hidden satellite's wires.

And the extroverted one, who doesn't like to cook,
takes the blond wig and drags it on the floor for the others,
like SAVAK yanking Khomeini from the country by his hair.

AK, a Figurehead of the Revolution, Interviews the Author

AK: Upon whose authority do you say such
blasphemy against God, the Republic, and
my own decree?

Author: I pledge allegiance to the flag of XXXXXXXXX.
Furthermore, my own conscience compels me
to call you out on your XXXXX, your XXXXX of
women. Let me then answer your question with
a question: XXX XXXXX XXXXXX XXXXXX
the right to decree?

AK: Can you tell me why a man of my stature should
even bother listening to some inconsequential
hack? You bark like a puppy dog of that greater
bitch, Salman Rushdie.

Author: God has sent me to speak for the unheard,
including my own family who you XXXX
XXXXX XXXX, and after XXXXX, lied about
XXXX.

AK: Little infidel born of the Great Satan who can't
even attest to being Muslim, how can you claim
to speak the truth?

Author: XXXX XXXXXXX XXXXXX! XXX XXXX by the
resistance to censorship?

AK: I have been dead several years, yet I am made to speak here. Just who censors whom?

Author: Your Excellency, I let you speak here for our readers. Yet even beyond the grave, you won't let me say a word.

AK: Heaven will show no mercy on you.

Author: XXXX XXXX XXXX by the will of God.

Eating Chelo at Aunt Behjat's in Tehran

Before the soldiers came for her brother
I watched my aunt cooking basmati rice.
When she lifted the rattling steel cover,
A burst of steam ran makeup down her eyes.
Under the faucet she massaged the grain
Then recooked it in oil to form a skin;
A pinch of saffron bled a yellow stain
On the thumbnail she used to scratch her chin.
While digging all the rice out of the pot,
She tried a spoonful covered with sumac;
On her top lip a single grain was caught
Like red lipstick clumped deep in a dry crack.
As she carried the plate to get the door,
I watched her pale face painted in horror.

Prelude to a Blackout

The peddler rolls his cart to another part of town.
The bee, stumbling from a cloud of teargas, burns in the
    garden.
Yet the city at twilight reveals flickers of hope.
In the twenty-first century, the greatest revolutions
are fought via satellite. As the crescent moon reddens
to mark the day's freshly scrubbed streets,
television beams into homes made of mud,
anointing postmodern cave dwellers with its secret of fire.
Perhaps Mohammad, a man sick of the world
selling the soul through illusion, could see beyond
commercial hypocrisy, and into the nature of things.
Assume that the omnipresent Allah
(all praise and glory to his name) appears to people
in the medium that best captures the spirit of the age.
Picture amidst so many images of sex on sale
the viewer becoming a channel for the divine,
a momentary frame of reality compelling believers
to raise swords against a sea of falsely bearded men
who come with scissors to cut the wires.

Iranian Darwins

Knives in bushes, man-made thorns so striking
they draw rose blood, arterial angels
on the sidewalk, faces heavy with frost
falling to splashes of life in the spring.
So the fate of Persian writers: cutthroat
competition for the national ear
breeding fuller Shirazi "boom booms!" hearts
exploding in old neighborhoods, bearded
Muslims, Iranian Darwins seeing
an end to certain characters who fail
to follow the revolution, discordant
cadence rejected, reduced to flat line.
Heading home with poems from my uncle
Tucked in my coat, I slipped on ice and fell.

At the Hezbollah Recruiting Station

Except for the posters of suicide bombers
it could be a pup tent along the highway;
the overblown painting of Nasrallah
might pass for a kind of Cub Scout leader

overseeing the preteenaged boys who hand out leaflets
and little candies on the days scores die from a missile
that could just as well be a harmless celebration
like *Eid-al-Fitr* or Imam Ali's birthday.

It's almost nap-time. The shutters,
like everyone's eyes (which, we learn from science,
haven't changed size since childhood), begin closing.
Like dawn in the Koran, when light and dark threads

become distinguishable,
the time between dreams and strong tea
becomes an unconscious recollection of the self:
first the face, tired of masking true feelings,

surrenders.
The extremities follow.
Across the region millions of husbands and wives
make love as children sleep.

This is how they were made, these boys;
except for the posters above them,
images of their future,
this is who they remain.

Dear Regime (Letters toward a Revolution)

> Why can't the beggar play the king?
> —*Hafez*

I've constructed these seemingly innocent lines
from wire in the basement of my New Jersey home.
Shebang!
You're dead. Or at least pretend dead
the way children die
for a few seconds on the playground.
I'm king for a day, or at least for a moment
the way most kings ruled the country
with little thought of longevity.
Hear-ye, Hear-ye: the crown decrees
a return to true freedom;
permission to say this, that, or the other thing
sets a train of circumstances in motion
much like letters in a book.
Before reading it, the reader's preconceptions
have disintegrated into thin air.
"All aboard!" says the writer
in retrospect, wearing the conductor's hat.
"Shebang!"
(So to speak)
a bomb engineered in the spirit
of a literary revolution.

Revolutionary Reflections

for Barry Rosen

The young idealists who stormed the embassy
now fear their twenty-something children
will fight some useless war.
Better to progress in the Western world
represented by the ideal of a free country.
How's this for full circle?
The blindfolded teaching the veiled to see.
Ex-hostages, once unshaven for 444 days
look to the bathroom mirror in their latter years
much like the smooth-faced ex-revolutionaries
who, from time to time, reflect on their youth.
"What were we thinking?" they ask.
Meanwhile, the wheels of army trucks keep turning,
destined to carry a country
in a meaningless direction
where few really want to go.

Part B(ut Poetry Doesn't Make Revolutions)

Essential Journey

This is the part in the book where things could go either way:
I stand on line at the ticket counter
choosing between Mecca and the long ride home.

This is the point at which the reader may abandon the
      narrative
and flip through pages, making the train move
with such celerity that the passerby . . .

This is where the writer risks wearing the conductor's hat,
choo-chooing his way through discovery with a statement like
"My name is Roger Sedarat and I'm really inspired."

This is the otherness of which we are so afraid,
source of both quest and suffering,
a return to true origins.

This is me coming apart at the seams
as a sea of Egyptian cotton swirls around a stone
to wear away the force of human nature.

This is this, that, and the other thing gone awry,
the phenomenological world in a hall of mirrors
stretched to its limits.

This process makes me crazy on paper
as opposed to the kind of subtle awareness
that my mind is not a reliable source of information.

This this this . . . stuttering comes from desire
for my parents' love, an expression stuck
in my mouth like spoonfuls of peanut butter.

This is, in the final analysis, a definition
of a man who, unable to speak for himself,
merely points where he's headed.

Flying to Persia

This is no nation for an activist.
Burned effigies of the colonizer
Assimilate into the incensed air.
The native language, having existed

Through centuries of invasions, survives
Demands for change as well as those clichés
Rewritten in a global marketplace.
When classic poems have been memorized

By generations, carrying a sign
Through the bazaar can only tire one's arm,
And so, as Yeats sailed to Byzantium,
I flew to this aesthetic land resigned

To see my life displaced beyond my will,
Transfixed within a universal scheme
Invented by forefathers; what I mean
Is what I read with so much time to kill.

A single couplet can retell my story,
A man paralyzed by parataxis,
Inhabiting that moment when fact is
Somehow surrendered into mystery.

Dowsing

I find a split branch to follow like a fork in the road,
my destiny to discover the greatest resource of the region.

Not for oil do I wire my spirit to the divine,
not even for water (though the desert remains dry).

Somewhere within ancient irrigation tunnels runs the blood
of my ancestors for which this nation still hungers.

When near I'll feel a twitch and dig spoonfuls of soil
with my little shovel, an archeologist resurrecting

the spirit of the place. To translate broken letters
overinterprets what they meant in a far different time,

building dinosaur models instead of living wonders
that once awed the earth. With a stick in one hand

and a pen in the other, I pray to intuit voices
of landscape at the level of simple nouns,

letting words stand for nature in primal origins—
water, fire, soil, and air. Oh, who am I kidding?

Like I'm that pure; like I could say X marks the spot
to shake hands with old masters and talk over tea.

The truth is once while camping on the way to Isfahan,
I saw a common bird perched on a cactus.

Thinking of the falcon and his falconer, I killed the bird
with my slingshot and a hundred-*rial* coin

(the price of culture crossing nature).
I felt guilty, yet strangely triumphant,

as if capturing the historical power of the hunting bird
instead of some common lark.

Qormeh Sabzi

As I stand holding her up,
Grandma Taj cuts the blue-green vein
from her arm and yanks it like a string,
pulls leeks, spinach, green onion,

and parsley out of her paralyzed side,
scratches her right cheek, the skin
from a white onion cracking
between her fingers as she rips

out an eye that becomes a dried lime
rolling across the counter.
The strike, strike of a wooden match,
the blue gas flame

under the bubbling pot, the chanting
of verses from the Koran.
I watch the miracle of saffron rice
appearing on a platter, her bleeding gums,

the pained whisper of *Allah-o Akbar*
through missing front teeth.
I sip the wooden spoonfuls of sauce
she holds in her trembling hand

and know the magic of blood;
I eat the piece of *tadeeg* she breaks,

the oil and turmeric oozing
into the grooves of her palm

and down my chin and I know
what it means to give oneself
completely.
She asks me to carry her

to the table, her body folded
into my arms, the nails on
her working hand digging
into my neck as if to make

another meal, and in the pain
I feel such guilt, suspecting
I have too little inside to give until
part of me begins to die.

Khomeini's Beard

In twilight the carpet weavers' threads change color;
soon the boys' fingers reveal behind the red-blue forests
deep indentions, stone calluses,
as they wave east with their bodies in prayer,
corn husks crackling in the wind that comes singing
through the teeth of a pitchfork left stuck in the earth,
the fire-building farmer dropping his wood,
the cupped curl of his ear, pink as a newborn calf, hanging
    on each word
singing in microphone static like streaks of lightning from
    Isfahan,
white Arabic burning above a mosque's
gold belly, the echo of an *Allah-o Akbar* rolling
like thunder, like clouds of sand on the village trail beneath
    the feet
of oxen, stirring doves from an olive tree, constellations,
each pair of wings flapping white and electric.

Doctor

How to tell the doctor
who specializes in treating opium addicts
his translations of Hafez need fixing?

Of a cedar stature. "Would you say it like this
In English?" he asks. "No," I reply.
"I'd just call her 'tall.'"

"But where's the poetry in that?" he asks.
"Somewhere in the nineteenth century," I reply,
munching on fried shrimp, watching my son play

with his son on an indoor jungle gym
supervised by Scheherazade, the maid's daughter.
I'd rather watch the boys slide

to pieces of fresh watermelon
and wave their hands while dancing in circles
to music on Persian satellite TV.

How to tell the doctor
without hurting his feelings
I'd rather hear about his real work,

the millionaire living in a high-rise
full of smoky dreams, staring all day
at the Baby Channel.

I'd rather appreciate the irony
of a country rich in ancient literature
producing an Oxford-educated young man

unable to tell the difference
between himself and a Teletubby;
I'd rather the doctor write this poem,

spending his leisure time on this patient
who reduces the potential meaning of life
to an undeveloped dream.

Thigh

With the honesty of homemade butter,
paddle-churned cream (*eshta* in Arabic,
ecstasy foaming to the brim), a woman
river-bathes, sheet of oil-black hair breaking
in rapids, cut lemon scintillating
olive skin free of tree-stumped chador, skirts
within skirts, peal of her bell-body rung
muffled in Iran heat—a splash of white.
The rhythm of pumice scraping her feet,
sandbar against warm current, frothy cape
a bee-bubbled hive, honeyed trace curling
to her bare knees, thick transparent lather.
At a Tehran bazaar endless gold-stores
could never place me anywhere so pure.

Haji as Stick Figure

In the world Haji finds himself
without depth, the shadow of a man
on the warning sign of a hot water heater
getting blown away, or the same figure
bumping his head against the roof of a moving van.
Always the impending doom ready to fill
his void with pain, a savior
without spirit, a ghost haunting
every conceivable catastrophe, wading barefoot
in a bathtub while blow-drying his hair,
sticking an arm into the garbage disposal,
feeding the ferocious animals at the zoo.
Always the fear of the darkness he's made
to inhabit, the representation of form
on the wall of a cave that he knows
would disappear in the sun.
Always the longing to fill himself in,
to brush light into his being and feel his own gravity.
Only then might he find himself able to run
from his eternally recurring danger.

Permissible Grapes, Forbidden Wine

If you're happy and you know it, Haji,
stomp your feet in a wooden bowl.
Tread over the ancient trope of your region
for a once famous family vineyard, now abandoned,
transplanted to Australia, subsumed by the name "Shiraz."
If you're happy and you know it
the verse you write will surely show it.
As the juice runs through your toes,
you'll sense the discriminating nose
of a twenty-first-century Persian poet
inspired to return to origins.
If you're happy and you know it, say "I am
that very poet." Stomp your feet and store the red
in rows of barrels in your head arranged by ancestors
who ask if you're their true inheritor.
If you're happy and you know it, say "I am."

This Little Haji

This little Haji went to market.
This little Haji stayed home.
This little Haji chewed kebab.
This little Haji gnawed bone.
This little Haji cried, "We little Hajis are all of us alone."

This little Haji pointed to that little Haji and said, "Same."
This little Haji asked that little Haji about the weather in exile.
I think we can see where this is going:
These little Hajis will seek connection for a while.
These little Hajis, for all their crying of "We," are destined to
    remain single.

But agoraphobic Haji insists on going to the bazaar.
But hungry Haji attempts a Ramadan fast.
(I think we can see where this is going.)
But this little fading Haji thinks that he will last.
But this and that little Haji will end up in the past.

"Bam Bam!" into things crashed blind Haji who's always in
    search of the light.
"Chug, Chug!" drank drunk little Haji stumbling toward the
    mosque to pray.
"Banal," said the reader who knew what was coming.
"Who cares!" roared hysterical Haji who called life a constant
    cliché.
"This little Haji!" cried this little Haji who never could get on
    his way.

Jun

(def. farsi: term used as a term of endearment for loved ones)

Allah *jun*, baba *jun*,
On my better days, when life itself becomes a blessing,
I walk with a suffix attached to my name
and what I perceive becomes a part of my poem,
naming the end of all that is dear.
Owl *jun*, in darkness the white mouse appears.
Mouse *jun*, as prey you do not see death coming.
I owe you, my father, a letter of forgiveness.
Baba *jun*, a kiss and a hug. Let our past,
if not forgotten, get in line behind the sacred.
Baby *jun*, in the grass my infant son
widens his eyes to devour the horizon.
June bug, attached to the light behind screens,
framing my childhood out of nowhere,
less romantically picturing what I begin
than doubling the absurdity of existing in time.
June *jun*, one summer month we fish as father and son
for each other in God, casting lines
into the horizon, making the night
more transparent than verbiage —
prose best representing what's elusive
and hard to explain.
Wordless *jun* wonder that leads me to love
with nothing so dear as your silence,
why must I repeat your end?

Adidas

Near the entrance of Persepolis
a couple of key players,
kings perhaps,
emerge from a giant stone slab
in full courtly attire.
Above all, the shoes strike me as modern;
fitting my friend Omid tells me
that he heard Adidas copied the style.
As we ascend the mountain to so and so's tomb,
I spot a German tourist in the same shoes.
No poet could've planned such irony.
Meanwhile, the guard in the watchtower
repetitively warns not to touch anything
as if he's learned, after so many years
to stop endless layers of graffiti
from soldiers in wars going back to the Persians'
fight against Alexander.
This makes the German's imprint
of the logo in the sand
all the more significant,
a momentary transgression
against the powers that be.
On my way to the parking lot,
my friend Omid informs me
they made the steps small
so the king could seamlessly descend.
Near the bottom, I turn to take a picture
of the German, who, despite being a tourist,
walks with a kind of royal grace.

Persian Haiku

Schoolchildren
smelling *norangi* blossoms . . .
spring morning.

Quiet nightingale!
You've landed on a mosque . . .
an imam chanting.

Sprinkling sumac
on the chelo kebab . . .
the call to prayer.

Haji's Rubaiyyat

Come, fill the cup, and in the fire of Spring
Your Winter-garment of repentance fling:
The bird of time has but a little way
To flutter—and the bird is on the wing.

— *Omar Khayyam*

I could rationalize the stars, Khayyam,
Make much out of the man I think I am;
My quatrains still would produce empty rhymes,
A song to hear but not to understand.

The bowl of fire once used to hold the day
(Now a subject of anthropology)
Is filled with fissures. All substance escapes
From every broken word I try to say.

The bird may very well be on the wing,
But there is nothing left for him to sing;
His throat is dry and wine no longer wets
His whistle to sound his inner being.

Is it enough to inhabit silence?
Is it enough to sit in the dark since
It is impossible to prove myself?
I've done the math and found I make no sense.

This age still mourns the absent nightingale
And would revive its songs: traditional
Sounds of nature where spirit and matter
Make music that means something beautiful.

The bird beak's screech like nails on a chalkboard,
The needle's scratch on a broken record,
Have overplayed the Persian romance themes
(Traces of which are seldom ever heard).

I should've been the song itself before
The Fall, when constructors of meaning bore
Their names by craft: "Attar" became "druggist";
"Assar": "oil presser"; "Khayyam": "tent maker."

Called "Haji," a name self-chosen, I've yet
To make my Mecca pilgrimage; I've yet
To make a thing of myself worth saying.
When asked, "What do you do?" I say, "I've yet."

Oh for the afterlife! Oh for the voice
Of Allah to tell me I have no choice
But to submit and save my hopeless soul;
I'd find myself with angels and rejoice.

But nothing is determined in this world.
My only fate is played out in the whirl
Of a dervish around an emptiness
That I inhabit but can never fill.

Take me as critic of your Rubaiyyat
Or else leave me as nothing, a whole note,
Blank oval in a song with no meaning
That sings of who I am by what I'm not.

When Haji Comes to Town

The militia will use the sword of Ali to cut off his feet.
The censor will blot out his mouth.
Thus will he drag a smudge of ink
across the busy streets of Tehran
as if to say who cares for meaning
when the old masters have set it in stone,
as if to stand on his inconsequential soapbox crying,
"I've been to the center and found nothing there,"
enduring the random appellation of strangers,
titles of "infidel" and "madman" and "spy."
All the while black blood will flow from his mouth
into evenings of endless horn honking.
Like a student kneeling close to his text
Haji will follow the blur of headlights to oblivion,
letting the city speak for itself, and so illumine
the common language of the marketplace,
living in glory of neon kebab signs,
gold Allah medallions flashing on teenagers,
and the pulsing glow of coal set in water pipes
at cafés where men curse over backgammon.
Thus will he turn himself into a mirror
to show those looking how to see.

Advertisement Proposal

<<Hafezzz Cola>>

(Put in red and white colors, but
somehow get across the red
of a Shirazi rose)

*Product of the Haji Babba
Bottling Company

Points to emphasize:

- There is none like Hafez, why even try.
- Made in Iran, the cola fails to taste the same elsewhere.
- Needs to work on different levels, a new drink yet traditional.
- Spirit of Iran in every sip.

The Hysterical Is Historical: An Interview with Haji

Interviewer: What do you see as your first transgression?

Haji: One day, when I was around five or six, I put Silly Putty on the Koran and took it to the mosque. After Friday prayers, as men began putting on their shoes, I stretched that most fundamental of texts beyond its limits.

Interviewer: Were you punished?

Haji: For years I received both lectures and lashes. Worse was the feeling of being torn between cultures, wanting to belong to the tradition I disparaged.

Interviewer: So you felt like Silly Putty?

Haji: I did.

Interviewer: How would you currently describe yourself to your readers?

Haji: I'm a four-leaf clover who's been mown over.

Interviewer: Both lucky and unlucky?

Haji: The story of my life.

Interviewer: Would you say it's also the current condition of literature?

Haji: Insofar as I embody such a spirit, yes.

Interviewer: Who are your greatest influences?

Haji: For this interview, Socrates. For the scope of my work, Holden Caulfield, Omar Khayyam, and my namesake, Haji Baba of Isfahan.

Interviewer: A couple of these are characters, not actual writers. This may be a touchy subject, but you are yourself an invention, no?

Haji: It is as you say.

Interviewer: Can you define your relationship to your creator?

Haji: Can anyone?

Interviewer: Point taken. Still, there's something different about you as a literary subject. What would you say of your author?

Haji: I figure this "Roger Sedarat" is much like Edmund Morris.

Interviewer: Reagan's biographer, the one who interjected a persona within the life of the president?

Haji: Exactly, which was not a bad idea, except for the ethics involved.

Interviewer: Do you feel betrayed?

Haji: Yeah, and more than a little disappointed. Unable to truly write from himself, the poet invented me.

Interviewer: He could have done worse.

Haji: Agreed. He made me a kind of Rumi with balls. Still, under the guise of artistic construction, I can't figure how either of us could ever feel like a real man.

Farrokhzad's Paper Hat

Lines along which to cut out the crown
of Farrokhzad, anointed for an hour
in the empty center of modernity's tragic circle
where meaning folds back
into itself. Beaks of nightingales
to snip adjustable notches. Poetry's still
the putting on of tradition,
but as acknowledged play.
Matches to a paper hat, ashes for staining
lyrics onto the skin: paper tattoos
for a fantasy of permanence.
We are running with scissors, cutting out words
at random.

Haji as Street Urchin

Awake to fan morning's bowl of fire
with yesterday's newspaper—
the ears of corn soaking in saltwater—
Haji sits on the corner watching the women

pass above him like black clouds,
accepting currency from the eyes of strangers
who read him the wrong way, a mere child
fated to be born into the cold world

instead of as a precocious young man
who understands them enough to record
their random discourse in his little black book
and turn it into song: "Ears for the professor

with too many papers to mark,
for the student at the local *madrasa*
who fears the record kept of his soul,
ears for adultery, for moonshine

at secret teen parties." At the end
of each day he's turned himself
into the richest man in town. He will grow up
to buy his own cornfield in the country

where he will reap and sow
in secret knowledge of darkest transgressions
destined to burn in the city that serves
as the center of the world.

Haji's Garden

Hear Haji practice his diphthongs
While tilling the desert.
A land to which no one belongs
Will speak in vowels, not words.

Emptied of self the sky widens
Beyond all reasoning.
His head in clouds moves horizons
Too far for him to sing.

Keen ears can catch a syllable
Suspended in an hour,
When the bee buzzes itself still
On the cactus flower.

But alone, knee deep in the sea
Of sand that envelops
The listener, wind whispers the bee
Away and meaning stops

Before Haji's hands, harvesters
Of "a," "e," "i," "o," "u,"
And sometimes "y" (a sixth finger).
Here, consonants slip through

Space. "Oo" for the desert moon,
"Ah" for the rock. Between
Them no correspondence of form;
Here, sound remains unseen.

If a Body Catches Haji

Donning a hunting cap with earflaps,
Haji registers at a New York hotel,

so far along the trail of text
he reads behind the name "Holden"

signed on his prepaid bill,
fully aware that the very idea

of an innocent day, the sun striking
the brilliance of children's faces

as one stands in the distance,
is illusion. But out of the darkness

of a lonely night after too much gin
the words come calling. At heart

all close readers are hunters:
to stand at a critical distance

is to place oneself at the threshold
of meaning, where children spin

out of the light, the way Haji
himself circles out of his darkness

and stirs his coffee at a diner,
or sneaks home to waken his sister

for enough money and love to stir
something inside of him into being,

some substantial presence able to stand
in his place for a while, long enough

to set him free and let him hold
the hands of children in a field.

Picnic

Tea is to saffron as kneeling on the rug
is to a history of kings on the road
erecting tents, roasting lambs, etc.

Back in the city, who will free the prisoner
is to the guard as what is written
on papyrus is to ink.

When Haji goes to the park the ants arrive,
drawing a line from their mound
to the basket of fresh fruit and cutlet.

The ants are to analogies as cutlet
is to rhetoric. The exponential burden of laboring
bits of ground meat on tiny red bodies

thus makes a text worth eating.
This is the story of Haji's hunger
read in the mountains on an April day.

It may indeed prove delightful
to put one's bare feet in a cold spring
after such an arduous climb.

Yet in the final analysis, it is only a test
of his verbal strength to view the city from the country
and try not to compare.

Tanboor

for Jeff Kennan

Does Haji carry an ax to be like other Sufis
Or to honestly clear the tree roots from his soul?

His name stems from a creator so tied to the terrestrial
He has prepaid for his burial plot.

At the end of the day, each journey to God
Begins in the darkest part of the forest.

Chop chop, Haji. Though not quite harvest time
Your field still needs clearing.

The great "I am" upon the headstone
Takes an eternity of strikes to break.

Welcome to the chain gang of humanity.
For too long you've played the missing link.

"Timber" to the things you thought you stood for.
Good riddance to the idolatrous x.

Did you think you'd fall so easily
With a huff and a puff and statements of intention?

So much sweat on your brow, yet you fail to penetrate
The obdurate bone of your being.

Insofar as you write what you know
You appear, like Sisyphus, in erasure.

The knee bone's connected to the . . .
Is more like it.

Grind yourself to powder. Add yeast and water
To make a bread for seagulls on the seashore.

The water is choppy, but that has nothing to do with you.
The tide provides clams for the birds.

Reinstatement of the Rose

It's time to reinstate the rose,
banned too long for its multiple meanings.
Without pseudonyms, the journalist has a nose
for his own noose. If only to adorn graves,

It's time to reinstate the rose.
In streets of Karballah, believers' blood
runs like ink for the divine. Hafez
would dip a finger to write,

"It's time to reinstate the rose."
How else can lovers signify
in gardens of broken glass?
With kisses too forbidden,

It's time to reinstate the rose.
The once stormed embassy is now a museum.
Students of the revolution are professors
of a thorny past.

It's time to reinstate the rose
and return the world to poetry;
the language that governs the heart
at long last needs relearning.

Part C(ontextual Notes)

"Dear Regime,"

Kebab kubideh is ground-meat kebab.

"In Praise of Moths II"

Mehmunis are gatherings in Persian homes that typically last a long time.

A jub is an aboveground distribution channel that directs water throughout Iranian cities.

"In Praise of Moths V"

Doogh is a yogurt drink.

Uncle N— refers to the author's eldest uncle, Nasrallah Sedarat, assassinated after the revolution in 1979.

SAVAK was the secret police working for the Shah.

"In Praise of Moths VII"

The green police enforce the moral code in Iran.

Abgusht is a kind of meat stew.

"Calligraphy I"

The artist alluded to is Shirin Neshat.

"Cousin Farzad's Wedding"

Jujeh kebab is a kebab made from chicken.

"Eating Chelo at Aunt Behjat's in Tehran"

Chelo is Persian rice.

"At the Hezbollah Recruiting Station"

Sheikh Sayyed Hassan Nasrallah is the current leader of the Lebanese Hezbollah.

Eid-al-Fitr is the Islamic holiday marking the end of Ramadan.

Imam Ali, as the cousin of Mohammad and Mohammad's first son-in-law, is considered by Shi'ah Muslims to be the first and rightful caliph of Islam.

"Qormeh Sabzi"

Qormeh sabzi is a kind of vegetable stew.

Tadeeg is the crunchy rice cooked at the bottom and around the sides of the pot.

"Haji as Stick Figure"

Haji refers to a Persian character, Haji Baba of Isfahan, made known to the West by the nineteenth-century British writer J. J. Morier's picaresque novel *The Adventures of Hajji Baba of Is-pahan* (1824), which depicts Haji as a kind of charlatan, much like Molière's Tartuffe. The character of Haji has since been reappropriated by Persian culture.

"Persian Haiku"

A *norangi* is a small citrus fruit indigenous to Iran.

"Advertisement Proposal"

For a background on this poem, visit the following online article by the poet: http://www.persianmirror.com/Article_det .cfm?id=792&getArticleCategory=41&getArticleSubCategory=3.

"Tanboor"

Tanboor is an ax carried by sufis.